IN THE BEGINNING

Resource *Publications*
An imprint of *Wipf and Stock Publishers*
150 West Broadway • Eugene OR 97401

Resource *Publications*
an imprint of Wipf and Stock Publishers
150 West Broadway
Eugene, Oregon 97401

In The Beginning
By Schaff, Thomas
©2002 Schaff, Thomas
ISBN: 1-57910-981-0
Publication date: June, 2002
Previously published by NPP, 2002.

IN THE BEGINNING

Part 1: Understanding Genesis 1:1-5

1. Genesis 1:1 1
2. Genesis 1:2 6
3. Genesis 1:3 10
4. Genesis 1:4 13
5. Genesis 1:5 15
6. Conclusion to Chapter 1 19

Part 2: Creation or Evolution?

1. Introduction 21
2. Two dangers 22
3. We must make a choice 27
   a. Physical death
   b. Chance
   c. Finished work
   d. No third choice
4. We must live with our choice 29
   a. The spiritual and moral consequences of choosing the theory of evolution
   b. The spiritual and moral consequences of choosing the Bible's account of creation
5. It is always a choice of faith 31
   a. Evolution is not science
   b. Evolution is a religion
   c. Two faiths
6. One choice is better scientifically 34
   a. Laws
   b. Observations
   c. Science education and scientists
7. Conclusion to Chapter 2 43

IN THE BEGINNING

Part 1: Understanding Genesis 1:1-5

The book of Genesis is perfectly accurate in all that it states about the origin of the physical universe. But its intent is to bring a spiritual message. God commands us to search in the Bible, including Genesis, for what it can tell us about Jesus and His gospel (Luke 24:27, John 5:39). Let us explore the opening five verses of the Bible with that in mind.

1. Genesis 1:1, "In the beginning"

We can think of this phrase as meaning "first." It is not the "first" (*echad*) of Genesis 1:5 or 2:11, as in the first entry of a list. Instead, it is the "first" (*reshith*) of Exodus 23:19, as in the start of a sequence of events with other events to follow. It especially means first of a series of events that lead to a specific goal or objective. In short we could think of this phrase as saying "step one."

In the physical sense, this phrase refers to the point at which the physical universe came to be. Before, there was no physical universe. The physical universe did not have an eternal past. But it did have a "beginning." To that we can add that the physical universe will not have an eternal future (Psalm 102:25,26, II Peter 3:10). It is true that this universe has been given a hope of a share in God's redemption plan (Rom. 8:19-23). But according to I Corinthians 15:44-50, II Peter 3:12,13, and Revelation 21:1, this present physical universe will be replaced by a greater spiritual one, a reality which we cannot and need not imagine or describe now. God is from everlasting to everlasting. After they are created, His people live forever (Psalm 102:27,28). Even people who are not saved have an eternal existence (Matthew 25:46). But the physical universe has both a beginning and an end.

The real message of this phrase is found when we compare it to the New Testament book of John. From John 1:1 we learn that "In the beginning was the Word." That Word was Jesus Christ, who came into the world to bring grace and truth as a Savior (John 1:14).

Does Genesis 1:1 declare the beginning of the Word, Jesus? No. John 1:1 does not say "In the beginning **of** the word." Jesus is eternal God (Titus 1:3 and 2:13, also Heb. 1:8). Jesus was there in the beginning because He is the great I AM, the eternal One. In fact, according to John 1:3,10, Jesus is the Creator.

Does Genesis 1 describe the beginning of the gospel of "grace and truth?" No. The gospel was prepared before the beginning (Eph. 1:4, II Tim. 1:9, Titus 1:2).

Of what, then, does Genesis 1:1 announce the beginning? We find the answer to that question if we recall that God sent His Son into the world to be the Savior (John 3:16,17, I Tim. 1:15). He could not do that if there were no world in which to enter. Therefore, the first step in the fulfillment of the gospel was to create "the heaven and the earth," because the physical universe is the arena in which the drama of salvation takes place. With that understanding, we can say that Genesis 1:1 refers to the beginning of the fulfillment of the promised gospel. God had a job in mind and Genesis 1:1 describes step one in a series of steps that lead to the fulfillment of His specific purpose (Isaiah 45:18, II Tim. 1:9, Titus 1:2). The plan of God was set in motion "in the beginning" and would not stop until it was completed, at which point the physical universe will have served its purpose and its existence will end.

"God"

The word "God" is a plural word. That does not mean there is more than one God, for the word "created" is singular to show that the subject of the sentence is singular. There is only one God (Deut. 6:4, Rom 3:30, Eph 4:6, I Tim 2:5). Instead, the plural form of the word "God" highlights the fact that the Father, the Son and Holy Spirit are all God, and all three were involved in the creation of the world (Father: Mal 2:10, Son: Eph. 3:9, Holy Spirit: Psalm 104:30). The preparation for the fulfillment of the gospel was that important because the gospel is that important.

Notice that "in the beginning" of creation there was God but there was no one else. All by Himself, God took the first step in the fulfillment of the gospel (Isa. 44:24). To put it another way, "in the beginning" there was God without man (Job 38:1-18).

From the point of view of the gospel, the reason that God was alone at the beginning, besides the obvious fact that man was created by God on the sixth day, is that only God is competent to prepare the gospel and fulfill it in the arena of the created universe. The absence of man highlights the fact that God did everything, independently, without the counsel or assistance of man. Salvation is not a partnership. Humans did not participate in the design of the gospel and they do not cooperate in the fulfillment of it, even in their own lives. In the beginning and always the gospel of salvation is without the deeds of men (Rom. 3:28, Eph. 2:9, II Tim. 1:9, Titus 3:5). The God who creates is the **only** Savior (Isaiah 45:12,21).

It is not just that men's contribution is unnecessary for the design and fulfillment of the gospel. It is that men are the source of the problem for which the gospel is the solution. One important message of Genesis is the failure of men, or more accurately, the failure of men when they act independently from God. Adam was created in God's image. Adam was originally perfect in a perfect environment. However, he was also created to be dependent upon God. Adam and his descendants were, and always have been, dependent upon God (Prov. 16:9, Jer. 10:23, Acts 17:28). When Adam was offered the forbidden fruit by Eve, he should have cried out to God for strength to remain obedient. Adam, at that moment, should have called upon God for wisdom and courage to help his poor wife. But Adam chose death! The book of Genesis reveals that a perfect man, acting on his own, will choose death. Adam's perfection did not mean he was independently strong. It did not mean he was independently wise. It meant he was right with God. But he needed God's help to continue to be right with Him. The book of Genesis demonstrates the fact that when men turn to a reliance upon themselves apart from God they will fail (Genesis 3:1-6). Wonderfully, God, who alone is wise and able, designed and fulfilled the gospel plan that rescues men from condemnation and the corruption of sin (Isaiah 45:22). Genesis 1:1-5 is both a description of what God alone can do in salvation and of what men cannot do to save themselves (Exodus 14:13, II Chron. 20:17, Titus 3:5).

This leads to two important conclusions. First, for all that God has done, He alone gets the glory (Rev. 4:11). He does not share any glory with men (Isaiah 48:11). There is no basis for any man to boast (I Cor. 1:29). Genesis 1:1 removes any basis for the pride of self-achievement of men. Men want credit and honor for what they are and what they have done. But the record of history shows that they are to be blamed for all the misery in this world. Men want control of their present life and future destiny. But the record of history shows that whatever men do is temporary and full of mistakes at best. Often what men do is destructive to themselves and others. The relief and joy is that "in the beginning" God is there preparing the gospel, and men are not there to mess it up.

Secondly, because God does all the work in Creation, when He calls people by means of the gospel, they must completely trust Him.

God knows His plans for His people and knows what to do to fulfill them (Jer 29:11, II Peter 2:9). People must not trust their own inventions to save themselves but seek the salvation prepared by the wise and mighty Creator (Prov. 3:5,6, Isa. 43:15).

"created the heaven and the earth."

The word "created" (*bara*) means to make something new that did not exist before (cf. Numbers 16:30: "the LORD make, *bara,* a **new** thing"; or Isaiah 65:17: "I create, *bara,* a **new** heavens, and a **new** earth"). For example, it is used to describe the creation of life in Genesis 1:21,27 (Psalm 104:30). The Bible sometimes uses other words to refer to the works of God. The word "formed" (*yatzer*) in Genesis 2:7 refers to making something out of material that is already there. The word "made" (*asah*) can mean to create, as in Genesis 2:4, or to form, as in Genesis 2:18. There are other words, such as the word *nathan* that is sometimes translated "make," but is more often rendered "give." However, the word "created" in Genesis 1:1 means that God created the universe out of nothing (Hebrews 11:3).

In light of the gospel, we can say that it takes the Creator to be the Savior. First of all, only the Creator can create **new** life, that is, life where no life exists. For example, He gives life to His own body in the resurrection in order to complete the work of the atonement (John 10:17,18). In another example, He gives life to sinners whose souls are dead in trespasses and sins (Eph. 2:1). Secondly, only the Creator can create a **new** heart that beats with a love that it did not have before. That is, He creates a heart that has a new motivation and a new affection. For example, He gives to people, who were slaves of sin and in personal rebellion against God, the heart to love Him and the desire to humbly obey Him (Psalm 51:10,17). Having saved sinners, He gives them the power and wisdom to fulfill their new heart's desire. God's people are trophies of their Savior who is a Creator (Isaiah 65:18, II Cor. 5:17).

The word "heaven" really means "heavens." It is not clear to what the plural refers. Perhaps physically it means the heaven close to the Earth, the atmosphere that we call the sky (Gen. 1:20) together with the heaven far from the Earth, the expanse we call outer space (Gen. 1:17). One thing we can conclude is that the words "heaven and earth" list the total physical inventory of the universe. As we read in John 1:3, "All things were made by him; and without him was not any thing made that was made."

The word "heaven" could also refer to the dwelling place of God (I Kings 8:27). However, we must be careful how we think about this. What can the fact that God "created the heaven" mean? Are we to understand that the dwelling place of God was also created? Perhaps it refers to the inhabitants of Heaven, such as all the angels that worship and serve Him. However, if we include in the word "heaven" the place where God is, then the phrase "created the heaven" is beyond our ability and experience to explain.

One emphasis of the words "created the heaven and the earth" is that all things belong to God (Deut. 10:14). The physical universe in which we dwell and all of its contents belong to God (Psalm 24:1). The spiritual part of the universe is His as well, especially the souls of all people (Ezek. 18:4). God is the absolute sovereign in the universe because all things are His. He made it all and He does what He wants with it (Jer. 27:5, Rom. 9:18-23).

Another emphasis of the words "created the heaven and the earth" is that God is bigger than and therefore distinct from His creation. God is not a part of the physical creation but beyond it. Therefore, nothing in creation can or should be used to represent Him (Ex. 20:4, Acts 17:24,25). Our affection and concern must be in heavenly things, not in earthly things (Col. 3:1,2).

The physical heaven and Earth as well as all they contain amaze, delight and attract us. However, as wonderful as God's physical works are (Psalm 40:5), this created universe is no more than a stage on which the issues of salvation are played out to their conclusion (Rev. 12), and is afterward removed (Rev. 6:13,14).

We should mention that this Earth is the **only** stage. According to Psalm 115:16, only the Earth is inhabited. That is, there are no other planets upon which different beings exist, beings who do not share in the Fall of men or their redemption. Many unsaved people hope that beings will be found on other planets because it would mean this planet is not unique. That would support their belief that the elements of the universe spontaneously develop life. But that is not so. Romans 8:20 states that the whole universe was cursed for the sake of the gospel plan that is being fulfilled on the Earth. God is perfectly just and holy. He would never curse any remote beings for an event that happened on one planet in this galaxy. To that we can add the fact that when Jesus returns to this Earth, the entire universe will be destroyed (Psalm 102:25,26, Matt. 24:29, Heb. 12:26,27, Rev. 6:13,14, 21:1). God would be unjust if He destroyed beings on a far away planet at the completion of His work on this Earth.

Sometimes unbelievers will complain, with a false display of humility, saying, "It takes an enormous pride to insist that this tiny insignificant planet in a remote corner of the universe is the only place where life exists. How could anyone think that little humans, wandering around on a little planet like ants, could be so important?" For one thing, true humility is displayed by submitting to the revealed will of God. Promoting ideas that come from our own interests and imagination is a display of pride. For another thing, any person who makes such a statement is totally focused upon this physical universe and has no understanding of the far more important spiritual realities. The fact is that the value of a soul is not measured by the size of the planet upon which it is found or the body in which it is housed. The value of a soul is measured by the great sacrifice that the Almighty Creator made by coming to Earth in order to redeem it.

In creation we just begin to catch a faint glimpse of who God is. In creation we begin to understand His majesty, power and wisdom. And as we continue in Genesis, we begin to understand His love (I John 4:8). Think of it. There is only one eternal God. Forever there is God, a loving Father. Without end there is God, a loving Son. For eternity past and future, there is God, a loving Holy Spirit. He alone deserves to be loved and He alone has the capacity to love. Therein is the one great message: God loves Himself. The Father loves the Son with a great love. The Son loves the Father and the Holy Spirit honors the Father and the Son. They are a perfect society, complete, needing no one else. One perfect God. And yet ..... and yet ..... we read, "God created." Needing nothing and no one, God still had His creation at heart. We exist not because God was lonely or bored, not because He is a show-off, but because God wanted us to exist. He greatly cared for and continues to care for our souls. That love takes our breath away. Can we really grasp such love?

2. Genesis 1:2, "And the earth was without form, and void; And darkness was upon the face of the deep."

There is no physical counterpart we know of to which we can compare the image these words describe. This point in creation is beyond our experience and any physical explanation of these words is pointless speculation. Nevertheless, there is one fact about the physical universe we should mention that these words bring to mind. Whatever shapeless form or indescribable appearance the universe originally may have had, we know that the universe existed then and the universe with which we are presently familiar continues to exist today because Jesus holds it together by His will, partially expressed through His natural laws (Col. 2:17, Heb. 1: 3).

The spiritual intent of the words "without form and void" are best understood by comparing them to Jeremiah 4:23. In Jeremiah the words describe the foolish nation of Israel that had no understanding to do good, but were wise to do evil. However, more than being a picture of their apostate spiritual character, the words also describe God's reaction to their sin. According to Jeremiah 4:26, which is part of the context of verse 23, the words "without form and void" are part of a description of the results of God's "fierce anger." The word "darkness" is understood by comparing it to verses such as Joel 2:1,2, Zephaniah 1:14,15 and Jude 13. Clearly, the words "without form and void" and the word "darkness" point to God's judgment, to His wrath, and ultimately to Hell.

We do not mean to imply that judgment existed at this point in the history of the physical universe. After all, sin and its effects as well as its penalty did not become an issue until after humans were created. It is just that God describes the physical creation of the universe by means of the words "without form and void" and the word "darkness" in order to highlight His wrath, as He begins to draw a picture of the gospel message. Inasmuch as wrath comes because of sin, we see that Genesis 1:2 describes the reason for the gospel of salvation. The gospel is not designed and fulfilled to make people feel better or be more successful in this physical world. The gospel is intended to meet a far greater need, namely, to escape the wrath and judgment of God.

Notice that the verse does not say that "the heaven and the earth was without form and void." Verse 1 states that "the heaven" was created with the earth. But verse 2 excludes "the heaven" from its awful description. Perhaps the omission of "the heaven" from verse 2 is a picture of what we read in Ecclesiastes 5:2, "God is in heaven and thou upon the earth." From Genesis 1:2 we learn that the tragedy and horror described by the words "without form and void" and the word "darkness" is found in the Earth and not in Heaven. Perhaps the idea in Genesis 1:2 is that the problem is Earth's problem and not Heaven's problem. We mean by this that all the blame for the mess is to be found on the Earth and not in Heaven. God gets the credit for sending His curse into the world as a just response to sin. However, man who dwells on Earth must be blamed for the curse upon the universe and the judgment upon his soul. It is all man's fault. The blame cannot be charged to God of Heaven. Men try to blame God (Rom. 3:1-8). But it won't work. God is in Heaven and the sin is found on Earth. God is not limited to a place called Heaven, but in Genesis 1:2 the emphasis is that God is in Heaven in the sense that He cannot be accused of being an accomplice to Adam's sin, which he did on Earth.

The absolutely amazing aspect of the gospel is that, in grace, God decided to make Earth's problem His own problem, too. It does not have to be His problem, but in love He not only entered into this sinful world in the person of Jesus and took upon Himself the burdens of His people (Matthew 8:16,17), He also took upon Himself the penalty that His people's sin deserved (I Peter 2:22-25). However, we are getting ahead of the story. Let us leave this wonder for the following verses.

In Isaiah 45:7 we read, "I (God) ..... create darkness." One implication of this statement is that darkness did not exist until God made it, but it did exist after He created it. It is as if darkness had some substance of its own. From a physical point of view, we do not have an idea of what it means that God created darkness. There is no physical counterpart to this statement that we can imagine. By our common observation we have learned that darkness is the absence of light and does not have a physical nature of its own. Therefore, this statement must be understood spiritually. In support of that point of view, the context Isaiah 45 links the word "darkness" to the "evil" of God's wrath upon sinners. The message of Isaiah 45 is that God is God, totally in control at all times, including times of destruction. In other words, sinners do not punish themselves, in a kind of penance in order to merit restoration with God. Rather, judgment comes from the God of Heaven (Rom. 1:18). God has determined what is the just payment for sin and He alone sees to it that the payment is made.

Notice that verse 2 does not say darkness was "upon the deep." Instead it says "upon the face of the deep." A face identifies someone as a unique person, an individual distinct from all other people. Even God speaks of Himself as having a face (Exodus 33:20). The idea seems to be that the judgment of God is not on sin as a concept, but on specific people who sin. Sin by itself is not an independent force or an alien being that must be judged. Rather sin is a person's deliberate disobedience to God (I John 3:4). Therefore, it is the soul that sins which must die (Ezek. 18:4). The frightening truth is that Hell is full of faces, full of real individual people who endure the wrath of God because they personally hate God and rebel against Him.

These words "without form and void" as well as the word "darkness" can also be thought of as a description of the wicked earthly life of sinners who are in need of the gospel of grace (Prov. 4:19). First of all, they are "without form," or full of "vanity" as the words are translated in Isaiah 40:17,23. This means unsaved sinners are vain; that is, they are full of pride and their own selfish desires. Secondly, they are "void," or "emptiness," as the word is used in Isaiah 34:11. This means unsaved sinners have empty minds, that is, they have no wisdom or purpose (Rom. 1:22, James 1:6). This also means unsaved sinners have empty souls; that is, they have no goodness or righteousness (Rom. 3:12). Thirdly, they live in "darkness" (Prov. 4:19, Eccl. 2:14, Eph 5:11, I John 2:9-11). This means unsaved sinners hate the truth and all that is good. They rebel against any control and hope that the darkness will hide them from the searching eye of their Creator. And they eagerly seek to draw others into their dark, evil ways (Rom. 1:30-32). Men live in "darkness" not only because that is where they belong, but also because that is where they want to be (John 3:19). Men do not want to hear or see the words that tell them about their sin and warn them of the judgment they deserve (John 3:20). Sadly, the words "without form and void" as well as the word "darkness" describe unsaved sinners brief and wasted lives (Deut. 28:29, Eccl. 1:14, 2:22,23, I Tim. 6:4,5, James 4:14).

We should briefly mention that some people have insisted the words "without form and void," as well as the word "darkness," refer to an actual physical destruction of the world. It is their opinion that God's wrath was displayed some time before the description of His curse in Genesis 3. Based upon that notion, they say that there is a big time gap between Genesis 1:1, which describes a perfect universe and Genesis 1:2, which they insist describes its physical ruin. Their objective is to maintain the Bible's prominent place in their lives and at the same time fit within that gap the millions of years required by the theory of evolution. But that line of thinking is wrong. As we shall see in the second part of this booklet, it is not possible to make any accommodation for the theory of evolution and at the same time preserve the authority of the Bible. Genesis 1:2 is not a description of physical destruction. It is not clear to what it refers physically. But it is clear that it is a picture, and only a picture, of the spiritual destruction which accompanies sin. In addition to that, Genesis 1:31 states that God was pleased with the physical universe described in chapter 1. Therefore, Genesis 1:2 refers to a time when the physical universe had not yet experienced God's wrath.

As we entitled Genesis 1:1 "God without man," so we could entitle this half of Genesis 1:2 as "man without God." It is not that men who live on the Earth could ever be without God, for this is God's universe and He is everywhere present. Rather, it is in the sense of Ephesians 2:12, which explains that unbelievers, people who live under the curse of God and under the threat of Judgment and eternal wrath in Hell, are "without God" in this world, that is, without God as their Savior.

"And the Spirit of God moved upon the face of the waters."

The word "face" is the same as in the previous phrase, again referring to persons. The word "waters" can refer to several different things. Sometimes the word "water" can refer to judgement (Genesis 6:17). Sometimes the word "water" can refer to blessing (Genesis 24:17). But since it is in context with the word "face," it can be understood in Genesis 1:2 to refer to the people of the world, as it is used in Revelation 17:15.

The word translated "moved" occurs only here and in two other places. In Jeremiah 23:9 the word is translated as "shake." There it refers to Jeremiah's alarm and sorrow because of the sin of Judah and Israel. We learn from this comparison that there is no joy in the heart of God in the fact that sinners must be punished (Ezek. 33:11). In Deuteronomy 32:11 the word is translated as "fluttereth." There it refers to the loving concern a mother eagle has for her children. We learn from this comparison that God cares for sinners who are in need as a father lovingly cares for specific people whom He knows, that is, for His own dear children (Matt. 10:29-31).

Of the three persons of God, the Spirit of God is highlighted in Genesis 1:2. Though the Father and the Son share the concern for God's people, the reference to the Holy Spirit is used because God applies the blessings of the gospel to His people through the Spirit (John 3:5, Rom 8:9-16, I Cor. 6:11).

The amazing thing is that, after describing His wrath which ought to justly come upon all people, we immediately read about His gracious response to the sin of men. It is as if God, because of His great love for His people, can't wait to get started in rescuing them. The "beginning" came as soon as possible. That is more than anyone could imagine or hope for. We could entitle this half of verse 2 as "God cares for man."

3. Genesis 1:3

The next three verses could be entitled "God with man," in the sense that they describe the work of God in restoring men to Himself.

"And God said,"

When we open the Bible, suddenly God is there, all by Himself. In the beginning we start with a mystery: God and His gospel (I Cor. 2:7). How can we comprehend Him or His holy and wise plans? His eternity, uniqueness, majesty and infinite creative power are beyond us. We can try to understand how people think and act. But God's ways are incomprehensible to us (Isaiah 55:8,9, Rom. 11:33). And yet ... and yet ... we read in verse 3 that "God said." These words mean, among other things, that we were created to hear the voice of God, not as a curiosity, but in loving response to His message of love. Whatever we know about God and His ways is a revelation to us. It has to be because we cannot invent or deduce what God has in mind (I Cor. 2:9-14). Therefore, "God said" in Genesis that He began to fulfill His gospel plan in the universe He created for that purpose. "God said" in the Bible all He needed to say about creation and salvation so that we can be saved and love Him in return (I John 4:10,19).

The words "And God said" focus upon the important place that God's Word has in the economy of the gospel. For one thing, in God's Word we meet His power. God's Word is powerful enough to create (Psalm 33:6, 148:5) and to save (Rom. 1:16).

Secondly, the words "And God said" reveal His authority. The justification of sinners rests upon the decree of the Judge. He must declare them just if they are to be acquitted of their crimes against God's law. God has the authority to declare that. But the declaration of God is not like the pardon given by an earthly judge or ruler, which may be based upon a personal whim of kindness, or an indulgence. What God says must be right. The reason is that He is just and Holy. What "God said" in the gospel about the salvation of sinners is true because God is also the Judge who satisfied the demands of His law. In order for God to be just and at the same time justify sinners, He had to put the condemnation of His peoples' sins upon His Son Jesus. Based upon that work, God has the authority to declare sinners just (Rom. 3:25,26).

Thirdly, the words "And God said" display the unique place of His word, the Bible, in His plan of salvation. It is God's plan that salvation comes only through His Word (Rom 10:17, I Peter 1:23). It is only when a sinner hears and believes what "God said," not just with his ears but with his heart and soul, that he is saved. It is only when a sinner hears and believes what "God said" in the Bible alone that He is saved (Rev. 22:18).

"Let there be light."

These words are quoted in II Corinthians 4:6 as part of an explanation of God's work of grace in the hearts of His people. The connection of Genesis 1:3 to II Corinthians 4:6 is important because it shows that our attempt to explain Genesis 1:1-5 from a gospel point of view is not our own private method of interpretation. It is what the Bible itself does. God testifies in II Corinthians that the factual history we find in Genesis 1 is a picture of the gospel.

Physically, these words announce the beginning of electromagnetic radiation of all frequencies, visible and invisible. This form of energy is part of the physical universe in which the drama of salvation is fulfilled. God uses this form of physical energy to fulfill His gospel program. For example, sinners need the visible part of this "light" energy to help them see so that they can read the Bible and believe. In another example, missionaries use the invisible part of this "light" in the frequency of radio waves in order to send the sound of the gospel "into all the earth" and God's words "unto the ends of the world" (Rom.10:18).

Spiritually, these words announce the presence of Jesus Christ, the Light of the world (John 8:12, 9:5). Notice that Genesis 1:3 does not say the light was "made" or "created," as all other things were (Gen. 1:7,16,21,25,27). Certainly the physical light was created. No part of the physical universe existed before God created it. But Genesis 1:3 does not describe the appearance of light as a created act of God. This is important because the physical light is a picture of Jesus, who is the eternal Light. And He was not created. We cannot tell from this verse when the physical light was created. Maybe it was the moment God spoke in verse 3. However, in order to make a true spiritual picture, this verse does not focus upon the idea that there was no light before God spoke in verse 3. Instead, the emphasis of the verse can be expressed as, "Let Light that already exists shine into the darkness. Let the eternal Light come to the universe that needs it" (Eph. 5:14).

"And there was light."

The words "and there **was** light" emphasize the historical reality of the gospel. There really was Light in the world, as there is today (Matt. 4:12-16). The gospel is not a philosophy or a fairy tale. It is real, as real as the sin of men and the threat of judgment upon that sin. If anything, the Light is more real than this physical universe inasmuch as it will abide forever, even though this world will some day end.

The words "and there **was** light" also highlight the obedience of Jesus to the gospel command. As light was commanded to shine, so the Light, Jesus, did shine. In other words, as Jesus was commanded to do God's will in order to fulfill the gospel plan (Luke 2:49, Heb. 10:7). He obeyed (John 17:4), even to the cross (Phil. 2:8, John 19:30). Based upon Jesus' obedience, light could then shine in the hearts of His people (II Cor. 4:6).

These words of Genesis 1:3 announce the love of God. The words declare that there is hope for people who live in darkness (Isaiah 9:2, 49:8,9, Micah 7:8, John 1:4,9). Wonderfully, "in the beginning" God's immediate response to sin was to command "light" to shine. This is a testimony to the fact that "where sin abounded, grace did much more abound" (Rom. 5:20). Sadly, when the light of the gospel shines in the darkness it is misunderstood, unwanted and feared by men, as well as opposed and hated by the powers of darkness (John 1:5, 3:19,20). Joyfully, God commands the light of His gospel to shine in the hearts of His people, and God's word is stronger than Hell's opposition (Matt. 16:18) and a sinner's resistance to it (John 6:37, e.g. Acts 9:3-5).

4. Genesis 1:4, "And God saw the light, that it was good:"

Light makes things sparkle and paints the universe with the beauty of colors that are a delight to our eyes. A sunny day is usually welcome. It warms us and replaces depression with cheer. Truly, even from a physical point of view, light is good.

However, God sees much more deeply. These words can be compared to Matthew 3:17 and Matthew 19:17. With these two verses in mind we can see that the light God saw was Jesus. God looked upon Jesus and saw a righteous sacrifice who is worthy of praise. Jesus is good because He is a pure and holy redeemer. Jesus is also good because He is good for others. That is, Jesus is the Savior who is beneficial for sinners. They sit in the shadow or threat of death, and He came to bring them light and lead them into His kingdom (Matt. 4:12-16, Col. 1:13).

"and God divided the light from the darkness."

Physically, there is value in both a time of light and a time of darkness. In the time of light, we can do work. In the time of darkness, we can rest. But in an eternal spiritual sense, while there is great value in the time of light, there is none in the time of darkness. As we have seen, light represents what is good and darkness represents what is wicked.

There are several important spiritual messages in these words. One message is that light is separate and distinct from darkness. Light and darkness are never mixed. There is never a kind of gray half-light. This means that the good, enlightening truths of the Bible cannot be mixed with the evil, dark inventions of men. For example, the account of creation in the Bible cannot be mixed with the theory of evolution. Or, for example, the truth that salvation is by grace alone cannot be mixed with the notion that salvation is also partly dependent upon the efforts of men (Rom. 11:6). God divided the light from the darkness.

Another message is that we must never confuse light with darkness. This means that what God calls good we must never call evil and what God calls evil we must never call good (Isaiah 5:20). For example, some people bitterly oppose the teaching that a good God would send anyone, including little children, to Hell. Some people reject the doctrine that sinners are dead in their sins and have no free will to choose to be saved. Some people deny that God sovereignly elects only some people to salvation. Some people are offended by the teaching that sinners are saved by grace alone completely independent of anything they do. Some people despise the view that Jesus paid for the sins of only His people. Some people mock the idea that once a person is saved he can never lose his salvation. The Bible teaches these things. But some people say these things are not true. They say that these truths, which are the "light" of God's gospel, are really "darkness." In another example, some people are in love with the notion that God loves everybody and that there are many different ways to reach God. Some people promote the idea that unsaved sinners have the free will to choose to trust in God. Some people teach that salvation is accompanied by physical miracles and speaking in tongues. Some people insist that God allows divorce and remarriage. Some people believe that women can take a place of leadership in church. They call these ways wise, compassionate and good. They say that these lies, which are the "darkness" of man's evil imagination, are really "light."
But God divided the light from the darkness.

One more message is that while light and darkness exist side by side now, they do not abide together in peace. They are not companions. People who are children of God by grace through faith have no lasting fellowship with children of darkness (Amos 3:3, II Cor. 6:14). There is no compatibility between those people who trust in God alone for their salvation and those people who trust in themselves. There can be no true or lasting friendship between people who love the Creator more than this creation and people who love this creation more than the Creator (Eph. 5:7-11, II Thess. 3:6). There is a permanent, eternal division between the light and the darkness, a division that was declared in the beginning.

5. Genesis 1:5, "And God called the light Day, and the darkness he called Night."

In the Bible, a name is more than just a label that distinguishes one thing from another. Many times a name describes the character or nature of something, as for example, Cain (Gen. 4:1), Abraham (Gen. 17:5), Nabal (I Sam 25:25) and Jesus (Matt. 1:21). As if in answer to the statement in verse 4, "and God divided the light from the darkness," God is saying in verse 5, "When I divide the light from the darkness, I can tell the difference between them. I know more than anyone the nature of light and darkness. I do not make a mistake in labeling the light and the darkness."

Therefore, the sentence, "And God called the light Day, and the darkness he called Night," is a statement of God's understanding and competency. We can trust God in all that He has done and continues to do to save some people and condemn others, because He knows what He is doing in order to fulfill His plans (II Peter 2:9). God is smart enough to create the universe and control the sweeping events of this world throughout the ages that lead to the fulfillment of His salvation plan (Isaiah 40:12, 20-23, 26-28). Can we trust Him with the salvation of our souls (Matt 19:25,26)?

The label "Day" can point to many things. One important idea is found in Psalm 118:24, in which we read, "this is the **day** that the Lord has made." According to Acts 13:33, that quotes Psalm 2:7, the word "day" refers to Jesus' resurrection. Why is Jesus' resurrection highlighted in this Genesis picture of the gospel?

In John 19:30 we read that Jesus cried "It is finished." Since Jesus endured the wrath of God, nothing else must be done to pay for the sins of God's people (John 17:4). But in I Corinthians 15:17 we read, "if Christ be not raised (from the dead), your faith is in vain; ye are yet in your sins." If Jesus died to pay for sins, why is His resurrection necessary? Isn't the resurrection an extra but not vital blessing?

To understand the place of Jesus' resurrection in the gospel of salvation, we must keep in mind that Jesus suffered **eternal** death under the wrath of God, the only death demanded for the payment of sin. That was the work He had to complete. Our salvation depends upon it! But, did He really do it? Yes, He did. And His resurrection shows that the full payment for sin was made. If Jesus was raised, it must be that He went all the way through the required punishment. Jesus did not take any privileged shortcuts and leave us with a liability before the law. If Jesus was raised, it must be that His sacrifice was acceptable and well pleasing to God. If Jesus was raised, it must be that He is God, the only one who could endure the wrath of God for all of His people without being destroyed. If Jesus was raised, it must be that Jesus has the power and authority to keep His word that He is the Savior. Gathering all these ideas together, we can conclude that Jesus' resurrection verified the fulfillment of God's work of atonement. His resurrection can be called "the last step" in a series of steps that Jesus took to fulfill His work as the Savior. The work of evangelism that follows His resurrection is the proclamation of that finished work (John 10:17,18, 17:4, Acts 2:24,30,32, 3:26). And the return of the Lord Jesus is the end of that proclamation on Earth (Matt. 24:14).

The Light came into the universe and did the work it needed to do. That is, Jesus came into the world to save His people from their sins. God saw that it was a job completed and well done. The morning of the day of resurrection showed that. In the words of Genesis 1:5, we could say that God saw that the Light was good and knew how good it was. Therefore, He gave it the name "Day" to advertise the fact that there is no greater good than the perfect completion of the Savior's work of salvation.

The label "Night" also can point to many things. From the point of view of Isaiah 59:10 and John 11:10, night highlights the frustration of people who walk in their sins. This is illustrated by the Israelites, who tried to obey the law by observing outward rituals. Spiritually speaking, they stumbled and failed to find righteousness before the law which "they sought" (Rom. 9:31,32). The word "Night" describes the lives of sinners as a time of frustration, because as hard as they try, they never find the light. Sincere, hard work counts for nothing in trying to be right before the law. In fact such an effort is a liability, because it leads to God's curse and Hell (Gal. 3:10). God saw the darkness of self-righteous rebellion and knew how evil it was. Therefore, He gave it the name "Night" to show that there is no greater evil than seeking for righteousness and not finding it, but finding condemnation instead.

The labels "Day and "Night" highlight the permanency of the natures of light and darkness. Light will always be light and darkness will always be darkness. If there was, is or ever will be any doubt about the difference between light and darkness, the labels identify them for all eternity. They are labeled once and for all because they will never change. Also, the labels "Day and "Night" highlight the permanency of the division between light and darkness. The separation between light and darkness is never-ending, permanent. The hideous and chilling fact is that those people who die in the darkness will never be part of the light. They will never have any hope. The reassuring and comforting fact is that those people who come into the light will never be part of the darkness (Rev. 22:11). Their eternal hope is Jesus Himself (I Tim. 1:1).

"And the evening and the morning were the first day."

Many places in the Bible, the word "evening" is associated with judgment and destruction, as it is used in Psalm 90:6. Or it can refer to apostasy, as it is used in Habakkuk 1:8 or Zephaniah 3:3. Many places, the word "morning" is associated with blessings, as in Lamentations 3:23. Or it can even refer to Jesus Himself, as it is used in Revelation 22:16.

With this understanding of the words "evening" and "morning" in mind, we can see how the order presented in Genesis 1:5 is important from a gospel point of view. The idea of the sequence in this verse is that the sorrow of sin and misery ends with the joy of salvation (Psalm 30:5). It is the end of the tale that matters (Ecclesiastes 7:8). God's people, who were in darkness, are now children of the light (Eph. 5:8). For example, Paul, who began as a wicked and hateful Pharisee, ended his life as a faithful and loving missionary. He who headed for eternal Hell ended up in Heaven!

The sequence mentioned in this verse reminds us of the rhythm we associate with the passing of time. Time is a part of this universe that was created in the beginning. We cannot fully understand the nature of time, nor grasp what it means to be outside of time, as God is. However, we do know that all things are in God's hands and time is a tool He created to work out His gospel plan (Gal. 4:4,5). Of the many purposes time serves, one is to reveal the unique sovereignty and power of God (Isaiah 48:5,6). Two other purposes of time are important to point out. One is that time serves to highlight the shortness of physical life on Earth and the vanity of material things (Psalm 39:4-6). Another is that time serves to emphasize the urgency of calling upon God for mercy while the gospel is still available (Psalm 32:6, 39:7, II Cor. 6:2,

Heb. 9:27).

Conclusion to Chapter 1

The physical creation fills our thoughts and senses. We are awed by its vast extent. We are fascinated by its intricate design. We delight in its variety and beauty. But the Bible directs our attention, affection and adoration to the one Creator and only Redeemer (Psalm 90:1,13,14).

Genesis 1:1-5 honors God as the Creator. He is the supreme Sovereign of the universe because He made all things. All things, including people, were made for His glory. He alone deserves all praise and worship for His wonderful creation (Isaiah 43:7, Rev. 4:11). But Genesis 1:1-5 especially honors God as the Savior. He is the Creator who saves His people from their sins. Sadly, Genesis 1:1-5 reminds people that they deserve wrath from God for their self-centered, sinful rebellion. God made all things good. The blame for the fear and pain of this present world must be put upon sinners and not upon God. Joyfully, Genesis 1:1-5 also reveals the deliverance from judgment. It describes the salvation which God designed and graciously promises to His people.

Our only real comfort and hope is in the gospel described in the beginning, in Genesis. We must trust that God is as wise and mighty as His creation reveals Him to be. We must also trust Him to be as competent a Savior as we read in His Word. We must seek God humbly because we are creatures of the dust. We must seek God contritely because we are sinners. We must seek God promptly because the offer of salvation that came to the world in the beginning also has an end.

It is a wonder that God planned for the salvation of many and described it in the beginning. It is a wonder that God gives faith to believe the gospel described in Genesis 1:1-5. And if we do believe it, it is a wonder that God's purpose for creation includes our own particular salvation. We have no greater joy than to know that the Almighty Creator will not forget or forsake His purpose for His work of creation. That great purpose is His work of salvation, both in the panorama of history and in our individual souls.

> *Thus saith God the LORD, he that created the heavens, and stretched them out; he that spread forth the earth, and that which cometh out of it; he that giveth breath unto the people upon it, and spirit to them that walk therein: I the LORD have called thee in*

righteousness, and will hold thine hand, and will keep thee, and give thee for a covenant of the people, for a light of the Gentiles; To open the blind eyes, to bring out the prisoners from the prison, [and] them that sit in darkness out of the prison house. I [am] the LORD: that [is] my name: and my glory will I not give to another.

Isaiah 42:5-8a.

IN THE BEGINNING .....

Part 2: Creation or Evolution?

Is the Bible's account of creation true? Did God create the physical universe out of nothing in six 24-hour days thousands of years ago? Or is the theory of evolution true? Did the elements organize themselves over billions of years into the variety of complex forms we see today? How we answer questions about the origin and design of the physical universe is important. Our answers impact our lives now and have serious consequences for our lives in the future.

1. Introduction

Part 2 of this booklet is intended for people who claim to believe in the Bible. One purpose of this entire booklet is to encourage and increase their trust in all that the Bible says. But we hope, in part 2, to strengthen their trust in the Bible by demonstrating that the Bible is accurate and trustworthy in all of the accounts of the people, places and events which it describes, especially what it says about the creation of the physical universe. By demonstrating the Bible's trustworthiness in its description of history, we hope to support their trust in the Bible's most important message, namely, the gospel of sin, judgment and salvation.

Another purpose of part 2 of this booklet is to encourage Christians to stand fast in their confidence in the Bible when they meet people who question the Bible's statements. We hope to help them maintain a strong, faithful witness to the Bible's message when they face challenges to what the Bible says about the beginning of the universe. There is an immense pressure placed upon people by the scientific, educational, political and publishing institutions to believe in evolution. Scientists publish long articles in magazines in support of evolution, and the majority of the public unthinkingly assent to what they say. But Christians must never be intimidated by the volume of words that evolutionists use to support their views. Nor should Christians be impressed by the prestige of the people who use those words. Christians must understand that evolutionists' objective is to reduce the Bible's credibility in order to dismiss its claim on their lives (Rom. 1:21-23). Unfortunately, many people who claim to believe in the

Bible follow the crowd and assume that what scientific and educational authorities say must be true. Consequently, they try to understand the Bible's description of creation in a way that conforms to evolutionary assumptions. That compromise is foolish. It is foolish scientifically because it leads to scientific confusion and error. Far more importantly, it is foolish spiritually because it leads to spiritual apostasy and judgment. Therefore, we hope this booklet can be a resource for Christians who want to stand courageously upon the Bible and its message of creation. We hope to help them to boldly declare that the Bible is true (John 17:17) and that all men are liars (Rom. 3:4).

How part 2 of this booklet helps someone depends upon his interest, the personal questions he may have or the challenges he may face at the moment. If someone wants to understand the basic spiritual issues involved, then sections 2 through 5 and 7 will be helpful. If someone wants to understand how scientific laws and observations fit into the discussion, then he may want to look at section 6. Even though section 6 demonstrates the scientific validity of the Bible's account of creation, it is not included in an attempt to convince anyone who doubts the truth of the Bible that it is best to trust in the Bible. Scientific discussions will never do that. Only the Bible itself has the power to create faith in God's Word (Rom. 10:17). Instead, section 6 is presented in anticipation of any Christian who would wonder if the Bible has any good answers to the claims of the evolutionist, and if there is an explanation of the origin of the physical universe that harmonizes with what we read in the Bible. Therefore, section 6 is not presented to answer evolutionists' arguments "in kind," or impress anyone with the scientific support for the Bible's message. Rather it is meant to strengthen the trust believers already have in the Bible.

2. Two dangers

One danger is that we think **too little** about questions concerning creation and evolution. Someone may ask, "Why should I even bother with these questions? The issue seems so remote and irrelevant to my personal life." It is true that normally we do not consciously think about these things. However, we all have an opinion or idea about how the universe came to be. One purpose of this booklet is to help us realize that what we think about these questions is important.

First of all, Jesus referred to the events and people mentioned in Genesis as factual history (Matt 19:4,5). If we claim that Jesus is our Savior, and therefore claim to trust and love Him, then His understanding of the Bible ought to be ours too.

In the second place, it is more than just whether our understanding of the origin of the universe is accurate. It is more than just whether our understanding of the form and function of all of its parts is somehow useful for our lives. What we think about the Bible's description of the physical universe is connected to the spiritual condition of our hearts. That is, what we think about the Bible's description of the physical universe is based upon and shapes our opinion about God's Word, the Bible. If we doubt the truth of one part of the Bible, such as its message of creation, how are we to know if we can trust it in other matters, especially in its message of salvation?

In the third place, what we think about the physical universe has an impact upon our morality and ethics, that is, what we think is bad and good, or right and wrong. How we answer the questions we posed as we began Part 2 of this booklet has an impact upon what we do and what we encourage other people to do. We will look at the moral impact of this issue in section 4.

Finally, we are commanded to give an answer to anyone who asks of the hope we have in the Bible's message (I Peter 3:15), especially since the sinful world's evolutionary challenge prompts many people to question the truthfulness of the Bible. That means we must seek to understand and be ready to present with conviction the whole counsel of God, from Genesis to Revelation.

Perhaps someone may react to the questions we presented as we began Part 2 of this booklet by saying, "But the whole issue is too technical for me. I don't understand any of it at all." Yes, the issue can be very technical. Concrete and specific facts as well as mathematical formulas can be presented to demonstrate the reasonableness of the Bible's account of creation by the hand of Almighty God. But the discussion does not have to be technical; and in this booklet it is not. In fact, the support for the Bible's account of creation is so strong that it can be presented in a very simple and straightforward way.

Another danger is that we think **too much** about questions concerning creation and evolution. After having pointed out the "importance" of these questions and mentioning that our answers to them have "serious consequences," it might seem strange to say we can think too much about them. What we mean is that it is dangerous to think about them out of proportion to other issues that must be more prominent in our thinking.

First of all, being overly occupied with questions about creation and evolution is dangerous because it may erode our personal walk with

God. We must be aware that it is possible, in fact very easy, for questions about creation and evolution to occupy too much of our time and attention. Even if our objective is to look at the physical universe from God's perspective, the more we seek to understand the origin and design of the physical universe, the more we must increase our concentration upon physical things. Unfortunately, this focus encourages the interest and attraction for physical things we naturally have as physical creatures. In addition, as we increase the amount of time and resources we spend to investigate the physical evidence in the universe, we could easily reduce the amount of time we take to study the Bible itself. And the time and attention that we give to physical matters could lead us to place a greater importance upon them than we would upon spiritual matters. That would be a focus on the creation rather than the Creator. We must always keep in mind that our Christian life does not begin with nor is it nurtured and supported by physical things, but by God's word alone (Matt. 4:4, II Tim. 3:16,17). A victorious Christian life that is a blessing to God and men begins with and is maintained by a focus upon the spiritual things found in the Bible (Col. 3:1,2,16).

Secondly, being overly occupied with questions concerning creation and evolution is dangerous because it may cause physical issues to be the center of our gospel witness. A complete gospel presentation requires an immoveable stand upon the Bible's declaration that God created the physical universe and continues to sustain it today. That is why this booklet was written. However, this is not really an intellectual issue but a heart issue. How a person answers the questions we presented as we began Part 2 of this booklet is a matter of what he thinks about God and his own soul and not a matter of what he thinks about the physical evidence. Notice that Romans 10:17 does not say, "faith comes by hearing and hearing by the word of science." Instead, the power of the gospel is applied through God's Word alone. In fact, according to Romans 1:20, the purpose of the witness of the physical universe is "so that men are without excuse." Rather than bring men to their spiritual senses and cause them to seek the mercy of their Creator, the testimony of the physical universe reveals their insane rebellion and prepares them for Judgment Day. Therefore, a proper discussion with someone about these physical questions, especially with someone who does not trust the Bible's account of creation, must be evangelistic.

It is true that Psalm 19:1 states, "The heavens declare the glory of God; and the firmament sheweth His handiwork." The physical universe is a display of the glory of God's creative wisdom and power.

Anyone who looks around himself ought to humbly submit to and worship the great Creator of all that he sees. But that is not what happens. For one thing, unsaved men **cannot** understand a physical witness which points to spiritual truths. The reason is that all unsaved men are dead in their sins, so they do not have the ability to properly respond to any spiritual witness (Eph. 2:1, Rom 8:9). For another thing, unsaved men **do not want** to trust the Bible. They believe in the theory of evolution because they **want to** believe it. Their rejection of their Creator is not a matter of science but of their will. They can protest that they believe in evolution as a consequence of thoughtful evaluation of the available information and careful application of principles. However, as we shall see in section 6, evolution is not an intelligent explanation of the origin and function of the physical universe because it violates accepted laws of science and conflicts with observation. Unsaved people have a bias that causes them to cling to the theory of evolution regardless of the evidence. The bias may be based upon unquestioned admiration of and trust in teachers of evolution. The bias may be based upon fear of ridicule or persecution from the majority of people who believe in evolution. The bias may be based upon a latent fear of God as well as an unwillingness to be held accountable to Him.

If a person, to whom we proclaim the Gospel, has rejected the Bible's authoritative explanation of how all things came to be and how things continue to exist, that person will never be convinced by lucid logic or compelling evidence. Only when a person is born again by God's grace will he turn from his sinful focus upon himself and this world, and have the eyes to see and the mind to understand God's creative hand in this physical universe. Only when a person has been given new life through the Holy Spirit will he turn from his rebellion and have the heart to submit to and trust in what God says in His word about the origin and appearance of the physical universe. Spiritual life does not come through the testimony of science but only through God's Word (I Peter 1:23). Therefore, our gospel witness must be centered upon the testimony of the Bible, not upon the physical evidence found in the universe.

It is true that some people have heard a presentation of the origin of the universe from a creationist's point of view, recognized the wisdom of that view, and turned from evolution to a trust in the Bible's account of the origin of the universe. However, the truth is that they were persuaded to change by the grace of God through the Bible's appeal to the need of their soul. Sometimes a person changes his view from evolution to creation at the same time that he is saved. Sometimes a person will continue to hold to the evolutionary point of view after he is saved. But if he is truly born again, as God causes him to grow spiritually and deal honestly with his sins, he will become more and more uncomfortable with the evolutionary view and eventually repudiate it. Whatever a person's spiritual journey, his change of mind is always based upon what God has done to change his heart through the gospel.

Thirdly, being overly occupied with questions about creation and evolution could lead us to waste a lot of time, money and energy defending the Bible from the ridicule of people who believe in evolution. It is so easy to react emotionally to an attack and allow it to create thoughts of anger or self-pity. It is easy to seek legislative, political or social solutions in order to get relief from the unfair treatment of people who despise the Bible. Sadly, those kinds of defensive attitudes and actions crowd out the message of salvation which should fill our minds. Not only that, we must remember that the unsaved people of this world are dead in sin and will not respond positively to the clear message of the Bible. Only the gospel, together with the power of God's grace, is an answer to the wickedness of men. Besides, according to God's economy as laid out in the Bible, believers may never win any political or social battle with evolutionists, because wickedness must increase until Jesus returns (Matt. 24:12). Our job as believers is to bring the message of salvation, supported by the message of the **whole** Bible, from creation to Judgment Day, and leave the results in God's hands.

We must always keep in mind the purpose of this physical universe. It is a temporary arena in which a much more crucial spiritual drama is taking place. God made this physical universe to accomplish His spiritual purposes, one of which is to glorify Himself through the salvation of His people. The rescue of their souls from the threat of God's wrath on Judgment Day and the release of their souls from enslavement to sin and Satan today are more important than any physical objects or events in this universe. What matters most to God and what must matter most to His people is that they know that they are saved and that they nurture and cultivate a close walk with Him. Because God uses His physical creation as a tool to fulfill His salvation plan, any discussion about creation and evolution must increase the preoccupation God's people have with the gospel of Jesus Christ. Any discussion about creation and evolution must strengthen the confidence, relief and joy they have in the salvation of their own souls and the souls of others. Any discussion about creation and evolution must renew their hope in the promise that God will destroy this sin-cursed physical universe and replace it with a far greater spiritual realm (II Peter 3:12,13), in which they will live with their spiritual bodies (I Cor. 15:53), whose design and appearance they cannot now imagine.

Finally, we must also understand that the explicit information found in the Bible is trustworthy but the implicit information gleaned from our empirical study of the physical universe is not trustworthy. What we learn from the Bible is without error, needing no revision or correction. On the other hand, our conclusions based upon the study of the physical universe are subject not only to personal error and prejudice, they are also subject to change as more investigation brings more data to light. Therefore, what we learn in the Bible is the foundation for understanding the physical universe and is the final authority on any subject of which it speaks, including the origin of the universe.

3. We must make a choice.

Either the Bible's account of creation or the theory of evolution is the accurate description of the origin, function and appearance of the physical universe. They cannot both be true.

a. Physical death

Evolutionists claim that physical death is a normal event. It is their view that death is part of how the universe works. Evolutionists insist that death is a necessary function which contributes to the change of living things, as over time, only the fittest survive. In contrast to that, the Bible states that physical death is not part of the original design and plan of the universe. That is partly what the Bible means when it states that the universe was perfect and good (Gen. 1:31). The Bible teaches that death came into the universe some time after God created it, as part of His curse in response to sin (Rom. 5:12).

Although the theory of evolution does not speak to the question of life after death, focusing only upon this physical universe, most evolutionists teach that all living things (plants and animals as well as people) cease to exist after death. In contrast to that, the Bible teaches that physical death is not just the termination of people's physiological process but it is an enemy of sinful men (I Cor. 15:26). Far more than just separating them from any blessings they might have in this life, physical death is the last event most people experience before they face judgment and the second death of eternal wrath in Hell (Heb 9:27).

Clearly, we cannot reconcile the claims of evolutionists with the teaching of the Bible. Both cannot be true.

b. Chance

Evolutionists insist that random changes of the genetic code, together with the selection of these changes over a long period of time, resulted in all the plants and animals we see today. On the other hand, the Bible states that every detail of the universe was created according to God's wise purpose and careful plan (Psalm 104:24, Jer. 10:12), and that He continues to sustain it today (Matt. 6:26, 30, Col. 1:17, Heb. 1:3). Either one view or the other is true. Both cannot be true.

c. Finished work

Evolutionists insist that plants and animals have evolved in the past and continue to evolve at present. However, the Bible teaches that creation is a finished and complete work of God (Ex. 20:11). With careful breeding, it is possible to produce varieties in plants and animals today. But the different breeds reveal the built-in pool of characteristics with which God originally designed living things in order to help them adapt and survive. However, there are limits to the variety of appearances and abilities a breeder can draw out from one kind of plant or animal. Furthermore, breeding never changes one kind of plant or animal into another kind. The reason is that God fixed the characteristics of living things when He finished His works at creation. We may choose to believe either one view or the other. But both views cannot be true.

d. No third choice

As we can see, it is not possible to take parts of both views and come up with a unified concept that reconciles them. Some people want to believe that God created the world, but are at the same time impressed with the arguments of the evolutionists. These people hold to a notion that God created by means of evolution. For example, some people believe the word "day" in Genesis 1 to be a long age. But the same word is used in Exodus 20:11 to mean a 24-hour day. Also, according to Genesis 1:12 and 16, plants were created a day before the sun was created. But a long age, such as a million-year "day," would result in the death of all plants which depend upon the Sun to live. The attempt to mix up the two views, an idea called "theistic evolution," is not fair to either side. We must be honest and choose one view or the other. We cannot hold to both.

4. We must live with our choice.

Our choice to trust in the Bible or in the theory of evolution shapes what we think and do. In other words, the Bible's account of creation and the theory of evolution are known by their "fruit," that is, by the attitude and actions the two views produce in the lives of those people who believe in them.

a. The spiritual and moral consequences of choosing the theory of evolution

People who choose to trust in the theory of evolution believe that there was no Garden of Eden, no Adam, no sin, no Fall, no curse, and therefore no need for a Savior. Also, they believe that, since the universe began billions of years ago, it will continue for billions of years more. They conclude that they do not need to be concerned about Judgement Day at the end of the world, and so do not need the protection of a Savior.

People who choose to trust in the theory of evolution believe that there is no God, as described in the Bible, to whom they are accountable. They believe that there is no one to declare what is right and wrong. They believe that there is no one to whom they must give an answer for their thoughts, words and deeds which differ from the ethical and moral absolutes described in the Bible. They believe, instead, that they can set standards for their own lives based upon what they think and feel is right in their own eyes. They also believe that standards which govern behavior between people are negotiable and are dependent upon the situation at hand. Furthermore, they believe that no standards are permanent, that standards which shape human relationships must change as times change. Their objective is to live selfish, indulgent and immoral lives, and they delight in a naturalistic, godless theory, such as evolution, that gives people the intellectual basis to ignore their consciences and suppress the truth of God's Word. Unfortunately, they are left with a life that has no meaning or purpose, which leads to aimlessness, despair and insanity. And even more frightening, they are left to face God on Judgment Day, when they will have to answer for all they have thought, said and done.

The theory of evolution recognizes the amazing complexity of human anatomy and physiology. But the theory of evolution teaches that a human is really just a bag of chemicals with a structure and function that is the end result of a series of random biological changes. The theory of evolution teaches that people are at best no more than complex animals. Therefore, we should not be surprised if people act like animals and treat others as if they were, too. In other words, evolution promotes the bleak perspective that there is no reason to care about the needs and interests of others because life is a battle for survival. Evolution cares nothing for the individual, but instead is concerned with the survival of the species. It teaches that the universe discards weak individuals as it relentlessly marches forward to an unknown destiny. Evolution, then, is the foundation for the ruthless and merciless treatment of others, resulting in racism, genocide, abortion and euthanasia. Some people have used the logical consequences of the theory of evolution to justify such horror as eliminating an "inferior" group of people for the purpose of promoting the survival of the "superior" species.

b. The spiritual and moral consequences of choosing the Bible's account of creation

People who by God's grace choose to trust in the Bible's account of creation understand that God is sovereign over the universe and that they are accountable to Him for what they think, say and do. Those people rejoice in the message that the Creator Himself, who could cast everyone into Hell for rebelling against Him, who could be embarrassed and repulsed by their weaknesses and needs, has instead sacrificed His only Son to save all those who trust what He says and walk obediently with Him (Rom. 5:8). Those people know God subjected the universe and its inhabitants to His curse in response to sin (Genesis 3:17, Romans 8:20-21). They also know that God cares a great deal about the universe. He has designed and continues to fulfill a wonderful plan for what He has made (II Peter 3:13). The Bible tells of God's tenderness toward His creation (Psalm 104) and His concern for each detail (Matthew 6:26, 10:30). The Biblical account of creation is a story of real hope because it tells us of a God who loves and cares for what He made.

People who by God's grace trust in the whole Bible, including the

Bible's account of creation, understand that God is their Creator and has authority over their lives. They understand that God has created them for a purpose and that there is real meaning to their lives (Rom. 12:1,2, I Peter 2:9). They see other people as unique and valuable creations of God (Acts 17:26, Heb. 2:6,7). Therefore, they are willing to serve God gratefully and care for others with kindness and sacrificial love (Eph. 4:32, I John 4:19-21).

5. It is always a choice of faith.

Science is the collection of knowledge based upon the study of **observable** objects and phenomena in the physical universe. Scientific analysis results in a **conclusion**, based upon those observations, which conforms to known laws governing the appearance and behavior of the universe. Scientific analysis also includes a **test** of that conclusion in order to discover whether or not it is false. Therefore, when we seek to understand events that occurred long before anyone observed and documented them, we are not making a scientific investigation. What we say about the undocumented past, whether based upon the imaginations of men or upon the words of the Bible, is a matter of faith and not science.

Some people claim that we can study history as science. They say that we can measure present effects of past events. But the study of the undocumented past is not really science because we can never know for sure if we have all the facts or if we have analyzed the data properly. We can never demonstrate whether our collection of historical knowledge is true.

We can make educated guesses about the past based upon the study of circumstantial evidence by linking possible past causes to what we see today. We can put those guesses together and call them a theory. That is certainly appropriate, and our theory can serve as a model to help us understand the past. But we can never verify the link between the past cause of present effects. We can make analogies by comparing events with which we are presently familiar to our estimation of how things could have been in the past. But as accurate as our understanding is of something that we can see today, we can never be sure that the comparison we make is valid. Studying a present phenomenon is science. However, applying what we learn about the phenomenon to an unreachable past event by means of an analogy is not science. It is a guess. Guesses by themselves are never science, no matter what we want to call them.

a. Evolution is not science

The theory of evolution is not scientific because it makes statements about times, places and events that have never been nor ever will be observed or measured by men. That is why it is only a theory and not fact. The question of what happened "billions" of years ago is not based on scientific observation but on assumptions and speculation. Therefore, the evolutionary view of natural history is a theory and can only be a theory. It can never be a fact. In addition, the theory of evolution is not scientific because the analyses evolutionists make of present day observations based upon that theory lead to conclusions that violate known scientific laws, as we shall see in section 6 of this booklet. Furthermore, evolutionists never honestly face a test but simply modify their theory to accommodate new information whenever their conclusions about the universe are shown to be wrong. That is, the theory of evolution is never held accountable for the many wrong conclusions it causes its followers to make. Because the theory of evolution is not scientific, evolutionary scientists must simply believe that things have evolved, and exchange a trust in God as revealed in the Bible with a trust in the inherent properties of material things.

b. Evolution is a religion:

The theory of evolution is a religion because it makes statements about God. Evolutionists begin with the scientifically unverifiable assumption that there is no Creator, that He is not necessary to the existence of the physical universe. Also the theory of evolution is a religion because it makes moral statements. Evolutionists teach that the material universe is all that there is. Since the physical elements from which the universe is constructed have no morality, they decide that there is no standard in the universe for judging conduct. According to the theory of evolution, the only guide of behavior is the need to survive, regardless of the consequences the struggle has on someone else. In addition to that, the theory of evolution has the form and structure of a religion. Colleges and universities are its temples of learning which preserve its sacred books. Evolutionary scientists are its clergy, who protect and preach its dogma in journals, popular periodicals and television programs.

Evolutionary scientists guard their theory with religious zeal. The passion and emotion with which evolutionists defend their theory against the presentation of creation reveals that they really do recognize the weakness of the man-made structure of the theory of evolution. Scientific evidence demonstrates that evolution contradicts the facts and that the Bible's account of creation is the more reasonable explanation of what we observe. Therefore, evolutionists must suppress the evidence which demonstrates the weaknesses of the theory of evolution. Evolutionists must resort to convoluted and contradictory arguments in defense of their theory, to biased and false presentations in support of their idea, and to direct attacks upon anyone who opposes them. Their derision and wrath is swiftly visited upon other scientists who "heretically" present the view of creation, lest those who teach creationism undermine the message of evolution and "pollute" the thinking of the masses, whose support evolutionists desire and need.

c. Two Faiths

Evolutionary thought is not an objective, neutral, unemotional scientific statement about the universe in which we live, but rather it is a dogmatic statement of faith motivated by a deliberately antagonistic attempt to suppress and supplant the Bible's message of creation by the hand of God. Evolution is a product of the deeply rooted rebellion in men's hearts. Evolutionists desperately cling to their theory because they seek some justification for their claim that the Bible is untrustworthy. They hate the fact that it declares God to be their Creator who has supreme authority over their lives. Nor do they want to hear or acknowledge that they must answer to their Creator for all their wicked thoughts, words and deeds. Therefore, the theory of evolution is a man-made religion that competes with and seeks to supplant the gospel of the Bible. Evolutionists insist upon the exclusive loyalty of the hearts and minds of men, and so does the God of the Bible.

In Hebrews 11:3 we read "Through faith we understand that the worlds were framed by the word of God, so that things which are seen were not made of things which do appear." That is, our understanding of God as the Creator and Sustainer of the universe and all that it contains is a matter of faith. We must trust that what the Bible says about the origin of the universe is true, the only truth. What a person chooses to think about the origin of the universe is not fundamentally a result of human measurement and research. It is not a result of human logic. It is not a product of human debate and consensus. A person's choice is a matter of the heart. It is a matter of trusting either the wisdom of man or trusting in what God has revealed in His Word.

Therefore, each man's choice of the object of his allegiance reveals his faith (Josh 24:15).

6. One choice is better scientifically

The Bible's view of creation is the best explanation of the physical universe because it conforms to the basic scientific laws that describe and govern the physical universe. The theory of evolution contradicts those laws. Also, the Bible's account of creation agrees with observable evidence while the theory of evolution disagrees with much of it. These claims are substantiated at length in many books written by scientists who have degrees from respected universities and who have experience in many different fields of research. In this short discussion we shall point out only a few of the scientific reasons that make the Bible's account of creation more reasonable and believable than the theory of evolution.

a. Laws

Scientists make many conclusions based upon their observations. As time goes by and new observations are made, their conclusions are compared to the new data to see if they are still valid. Sometimes they find that a conclusion does not agree with the new information. If the conclusion fails the test, it must be abandoned or modified. Sometimes scientists find, after many comparisons, that a conclusion appears to continue to accurately describe the appearance and behavior of what they see in the universe. When a lot of time goes by and their conclusion remains valid for all situations they can think of, they grow more confident in it and eventually call it a law. That law, which is potentially subject to revision, does not have an authority equal to the eternal statements of God found in the Bible. Nevertheless, some laws of science have correctly described the basic form and function of the universe so well and for so long that we can make a good judgment as to whether creation or evolution is more reasonable when we compare both views to those laws. Let us look at a few of those laws.

The universe is full of matter and energy which are constantly changing from one form into another. For example, when we eat a sandwich some chemical energy is changed into heat energy. When we ride a roller coaster, our energy of position changes into energy of motion and back again. There is a law of science that states, even though lots of changes can take place, the total amount of energy and matter before something happened is equal to the total amount of energy and matter after it happened. No new energy or matter is created or annihilated. In simplest words, this law states that you cannot get something from nothing. There is nothing in the universe to cause new energy or matter to appear. This first law has never been observed to be violated.

This first law might help us investigate transfers of matter and energy, but it tells us nothing about how matter and energy originated in the first place. In fact, this law does not even tell us if the universe had a beginning. However, this law means that if the universe had a beginning, it could not have created itself. It could have come into existence only because of a power outside of itself.

In this busy universe full of energy changes, sometimes things get close to each other or bump into each other and exchange energy or matter. During the exchange, some of the energy is changed into heat. For example, the chemical bonds in a sandwich break during digestion and the released heat energy warms our bodies. The wheels of a roller coaster rub against the metal track and produce heat through friction. There is another law of science that states if we observe something happening and record all the exchanges in energy that take place, we will find that the total amount of matter and energy is the same before and after, as it should be, but that some of the energy has dissipated into the surroundings as heat energy. The important thing to notice is that the heat energy can never be gathered together again or changed into a form to do something useful. A sandwich is used up and cannot be replaced with the same chemical energy, some of which has been distributed to the surroundings as heat. A roller coaster will never keep going forever. Instead, it will slow down as the energies of position and motion are lost to heat through friction. The conclusion is that, as time goes by, more and more energy in the universe is being changed into a useless form, that is, into scattered heat energy. This second law has never been observed to be violated.

One implication of this second law is that, if we wait long enough, eventually all useful energy will leak away into heat and nothing more will happen. The universe will be dead. Another implication is that, in time past, the universe had a lot more useful energy.

Evolutionists claim that the second law could be set aside if we consider a system in which energy comes in from the outside. They point to the Sun's radiation falling upon the Earth as an example. They claim that such an input of energy accounts for all the complexity we find on the Earth. But that is not so. Energy into a system, by itself, actually makes the destruction described by the second law occur more rapidly. Raw energy input, such as the Sun's radiation upon the Earth, breaks things down and does not build things up.

Evolutionists claim that a living plant or animal is an example of a system in which the second law does not apply. But that is not so. The second law is valid even for a living thing which uses raw energy and builds itself up. The living thing must work to counter the deterioration which the law describes. But doesn't that work show that the second law is not valid for living things? No. A living thing can do useful work only if it has been given instructions, which is found in its DNA, and if it has been given the mechanism in some of its cells, such as chlorophyll in plants, for changing the raw energy it gets into a form that it can use to grow and maintain itself.

The second law is an important companion of the first law. Together they are a big witness against evolution and a big support for the Bible's statements of creation. According to the two laws, not only is it impossible to get something from nothing, but also what we get as time goes by is less useful to us than before. In short, the universe is wearing out. In the image of a clock, the two laws together state that the universe is running down and it can't rewind itself. If it was wound up before, then someone else outside of the universe must have wound it up. That is, the second law says that the universe had a beginning and the first law says that the universe did not create itself. These laws point to the hand of someone outside of the universe, to a Creator.

We shall mention one more law. It is similar to the first law, but applies only to living things. The Earth is full of many kinds of living things, but we observe that living things can only come from living things. For example, kittens come from mother cats and corn plants come from the corn seeds of previous corn plants. Similar to the first law, which states that we can't get something from nothing, another law states that life cannot come from non-living things. According to this law, which has never been observed to be violated, life can only come from pre-existing life.

Evolution states the universe is becoming more complex and more useful. But the laws of science, together with the Bible, state that the universe is running down and is becoming less useful (Psalm 102:25,26). Evolution states that the universe had no beginning. But the laws of science, together with the Bible, state that the universe had a beginning, when it was a lot better off, more able to keep things going, like living things (Gen. 1:31). Evolution states that at one time lifeless chemicals changed into life. But the laws of science, together with the Bible, state that life can come only from a life-giver (Psalm 104:29,30). Clearly the Bible's account of creation is a better choice.

b. Observations

We learn the size, weight, composition, behavior and many other concrete and specific facts about objects in the universe through observation. It is true that what we notice and remember about objects in this universe can be affected by our prejudices, ignorance and lack of experience. Therefore, our observations about the universe are not as trustworthy as the statements of God in the Bible. Nevertheless, there are many observations to which we may compare both the account of creation in the Bible and the theory of evolution in order to see which view best fits the facts as we know them. Let us look at a few simple, common observations.

Our common experience tells us that objects and phenomena in the universe have origins and causes. We observe the leaves of a tree move and think about the unseen wind that blew them. We observe a forest fire and think about the lightning or the careless match that started it. We observe that there is always a cause to everything that happens or exists. The theory of evolution does not agree with that observation because it insists that if we could go back in time, we would never find a first cause but that all things just are, without a cause or a reason. In contrast to evolution, the view of creation is that all things have an origin. And if we go back in time, we would see that all things in the physical universe exist because God is the first cause.

Our observations also show that all phenomena and objects in the universe have design. Things in the universe display their design in their amazing complexity. Things in the universe display their design by their intricate structure and the provision given to them in order to fulfill a useful purpose. Things in the universe display their design by their interdependence upon each other and how they cooperate with each other.

One good example of design is the human eye. The human eye is made of many parts. Each part, the cornea, the iris, the retina, all the fluids and nerves, among others, are precisely constructed to perform a specific function. Not only must each part be made right, but also all of the parts must work together and in coordination with the optic nerve and the brain to enable someone to see. A slight change in any part or a slight change in how one part connects with other parts results in poor vision or blindness. One thing to keep in mind is that not one of these parts is able to see. An eye is really a collection of non-seeing parts. Unless all of the parts of the system are in place and working properly together, the whole system does not work at all and is useless. In fact, a sightless non-functioning eye is detrimental to an organism because it can be a source of injury and infection. This means that the whole system could not have waited around as a useless organ for millions of genetic accidents to accumulate in order to produce a complete eye. The only honest scientific conclusion is that the intricate detail and precision of the seeing eye shows great wisdom in design and shows purpose of structure and function. This and many more examples, such as a bird's wing, which is a complex structure that provides flight only in coordination with all the other parts of the bird, are clear witnesses to the creative hand of God.

Another good example of design is the amazing relationship between two kinds of fish. One kind is the small black and yellow French angel fish. They hide in coral because they are often eaten by larger fish. The other kind is the larger yellow-tailed Goat fish. They eat smaller fish. Goat fish sometimes swim near coral and change their color to pink. That tells the angel fish it is safe to swim out and eat the parasites which are attached to the Goat fish. The Goat fish wait patiently to be cleaned but do not eat the smaller fish. When the Goat fish change color again, the smaller fish return to the safety of the coral. This relationship could never have happened by chance because one kind of fish is a predator and the other kind is a predator's lunch. Furthermore, if such a behavior was accidentally learned by one particular pair of French angel and Goat fish, the new relationship could never have been passed on to following generations. This, and many more symbiotic cooperative relationships, show the design of God's wise, caring and purposeful work of creation.

One more example of design is found in the genetic information found in a DNA molecule located in the cells of living things. Segments of the long DNA molecule, called genes, contain instructions in code for making all the proteins a cell needs. The structure of a DNA molecule and the process that is required to make proteins according to the code they contain is so complex that it could not have come together by random chance trial-and-error chemical reactions. It is also important to know that the information in the DNA is stable. The genetic codes do have instructions for some variety, such as differences in skin color, body size and other physical features. But the variety is always limited. For example, moth populations can change in color and dogs can be bred to change in size. But the organisms are always the same. Moths are always moths and never some other creature. Dogs are always dogs and not half dog and half some other creature. The limitations in the changes that organisms display from one generation to another are a testimony to the built-in genetic variation, which is a marvelous design that allows living things to adapt to changes in the environment. That is, different breeds do not mean new information is created, but that some genetic information is emphasized over other information. The idea is that living things cannot evolve into something else because the DNA message limits the amount of change that can take place. Living things are fixed into kinds as the Bible states (Gen. 1:24) and in conformity to the law of science that states you can't get something from nothing.

Sometimes, but not very often, when the DNA message is copied so that it can be passed on to the next generation, mistakes are made. These mistakes are called mutations, which evolutionists claim result in new kinds of living things. However, years of observations have shown that mutations are either of neutral value or almost always harmful. For example, a protein that is too different from previous proteins, because of a mistake in copying the DNA instructions needed to build that protein, would interfere with the function of a living thing and possibly lead to its death. A mistake in copying the codes is another example of the second law of science we talked about before. A copying mistake is an example of a less useful situation in the form of a loss of information, just like a typographical error doesn't add a new message to the letter but makes the original message harder to read. Mistakes do not add useful information but are a loss of information. Mistakes do not result in a new message but distort the original message. For example, mutations in fruit flies always result in more fruit flies, many times disabled fruit flies or dead fruit flies, but fruit flies nevertheless. This is a testimony to the accuracy of the Bible which states that one kind of life comes only from the same kind of life (Gen. 1:21,24,25) and that life is deteriorating (Eccl. 3:19,20), to which the genetic mutational load that living things must bear is a witness.

Even though they do not help us directly answer the question of origins, we must briefly discuss fossils because the theory of evolution depends so much upon them. Fossil evidence strongly supports the Bible's account of creation and clearly contradicts the theory of evolution. In fact, the fossil evidence is an embarrassment to evolutionists for at least two reasons. First of all, in rocks that evolutionists call the oldest fossil-bearing rocks, are found fossils of complex life forms, such as sponges, corals and mollusks, much like they look today. Amazingly, in rocks considered even older, not a single indisputable multicellular fossil has been found. Therefore, according to the fossil record, these complex life forms had no ancestors, since the fossil remains of their ancestors are absent. The evidence agrees with the Bible which states that life in all of its variety came into existence suddenly. Secondly, according to the theory of evolution, the rocks of the earth should contain fossils of thousands of transitional life forms. In fact, if over millions of years plants and animals have been evolving, we should see more fossils of in-between types than fossils of life forms which appear distinct from each other. The fact is that there are no fossils of in-between types. Evolutionists are so desperate to find them that the few they have promoted have been disqualified or proved to be a fraud. In fact, the history of anthropology is, sadly, littered with dishonest claims. For example, the remains of one famous ape-man, used in the famous Scopes trial to support the claims of evolutionists who wanted to discredit the Bible's account of creation, was later shown to be a tooth from a pig.

There are many more observations we could highlight that reveal the truth of the Bible's account of creation and contradict the theory of evolution. Some observations do not point directly to the fact of a Creator, but demonstrate that the universe is quite young, thousands of years rather than billions of years old as the theory of evolution requires and demands. Observations concerning Comets, the amount of Helium in the Earth's atmosphere and the amount of nitrates and minerals in the oceans are a few examples of these kinds of observations. However, these kinds of observations point only indirectly to the existence of a Creator, so we will not discuss them in this booklet. Besides, as we have mentioned, there are excellent articles in other books*, thoroughly and clearly written, which present detailed discussions of these and other observation, such as the use of radioactive decay in assigning ages to objects, the validity of the Big Bang theory, the nature of the source of the Sun's energy, and much more.

c. Science education and scientists

Sadly, the theory of evolution, which is often taught in schools as fact, is illogical and contradicts observations. It is bad science. In fact, it is anti-science because it contradicts laws, observations and obvious cause-and-effect relationships. Also, the theory of evolution forces students to work under the burden of unscientific assumptions and speculations that steer them away from more productive lines of investigation, as well as closes their minds to more insightful patterns of thought. For example, not too long ago evolutionists considered many human organs, such as the appendix, to be evolutionary leftovers, useless and dispensable. For a while students of anatomy were taught and willingly received these ideas. However, more careful study subsequently has shown that the organ performs important functions. The appendix is now recognized to be part of the immune system.

In contrast to that, the Bible's account of creation promotes good science. Recognizing the clear witness of an intelligent cause of the complex and fascinating universe, Bible-believing students of science expect to discover order, purpose and design in all that they study in the universe. Also, they are interested to learn more about the Person who made it. True believers are curious to learn how God made His universe so that they praise Him for all He has done. It is important to them how the universe now works so that they can give Him the glory for all that He continues to do.

Incidentally, evolutionists claim that no real scientist would be a creationist. However, many of the greatest scientists have testified to their trust in the Bible and the God who wrote it. These scientists refused to follow the non-scientific thinking of people who have insisted on promoting the theory of evolution. Men of the past, upon whose work the science of today is founded, who believed in the Bible's account of creation, include Isaac Newton, Robert Boyle, Michael Faraday, Louis Pasteur, Henri Fabre and Clerk Maxwell among others. Clerk Maxwell was quite familiar with the claims of evolution and rejected it as a clear-thinking Bible-believing scientist. Many men and women of today have been trained in the sciences at well known universities and confidently trust in the Bible's account of creation, despite enduring the prejudice and slander of evolutionists. Evolutionists also claim that creation-scientists do not publish valuable work. But the fact is that creationists are denied publication of their work because evolutionists control the editing staff of all scientific publications. So creationists must publish their studies through private means.

Conclusion of Chapter 2

Even though the answers to the questions about the beginning of the universe are a matter of faith, God asks us to believe only in what is believable. There is no value in faith in itself. Faith only has value when we believe in what is true. Any notions men may have about the origin of the universe which differ from what the Bible states are inventions of their minds and do not correspond to the real world. What men propose about the origin of the universe is a leap of faith in stories that are unreasonable and unsustainable by scientific investigation. On the other hand, all statements found in the Bible, no matter what the subject, are faithful accounts of what is true. We should never feel that we must apologize for what the Bible states happened "in the beginning." We should never be afraid to stand boldly for the historical accuracy of the Bible in the face of the prominent and fashionable attempt to invalidate it by means of the theory of evolution. People who challenge the accuracy of the historical details of the Bible and its relevancy to men's lives are false prophets whom we must not heed.

As we have said before, our primary focus as believers must not be upon science but upon the Bible. However, we must remember that this is our Father's world. He who created the universe also wrote about it in His Word, the Bible. And what we learn from God's universe through an honest and accurate study of the physical world is in perfect harmony with whatever we learn from the Bible, and strengthens the validity of the Bible's description of the origin of the universe. It may be that we do not have sufficient training to answer every evolutionary attack with an analytical scientific argument. That does not really matter. A little child who trusts in all that the Bible says is far wiser than any scientist who believes his learning is superior to the Bible (Psalm 19:7). The point is that we can be certain that science is not a threat to a trust in what God says in His Word, the Bible. We can be confident that what the Bible says about the origin and destiny of this universe, as well as what it says about our souls, is absolutely trustworthy.

We can say with the Bible,

"By the word of the LORD were the heavens made; and all the host of them by the breath of his mouth. He gathereth the waters of the sea together as an heap: he layeth up the depth

in storehouses. Let all the earth fear the LORD: let all the inhabitants of the world stand in awe of him. For he spake, and it was [done]; he commanded, and it stood fast."
Psalm 33:6-9

"O LORD, how manifold are thy works! In wisdom thou made them all: the earth is full of thy riches."   Psalm 104:24

"Thou art worthy, O Lord, to receive glory and honour and power: for thou hast created all things, and for thy pleasure they are and were created."   Rev. 4:11

* For titles and sources see www.AnswersinGenesis.org

www.ingramcontent.com/pod-product-compliance
Lightning Source LLC
Chambersburg PA
CBHW061516040426
42450CB00008B/1645